Learn Python in One Hour

Programming by Example

2nd Edition

Victor R. Volkman

Modern Software Press

2nd Edition -- January 2018

Library of Congress Cataloging-in-Publication Data

Volkman, Victor R.
  Learn Python in one hour : programming by example / Victor R. Volkman.
      pages cm
  ISBN 978-1-61599-239-3 (pbk. : alk. paper) -- ISBN 978-1-61599-240-9 (ebook)
  1. Python (Computer program language) 2. Object-oriented programming (Computer
science) I. Title.
  QA76.73.P98V65 2013
  005.1'17--dc23
                            2014017288

From Modern Software Press, an imprint of
L.H. Press Inc.
5145 Pontiac Trail
Ann Arbor, MI 48105

www.LHPress.com
info@LHPress.com

toll free USA/CAN: 888-761-6268
FAX: 734-663-6861

Contents

Dedicated to the Computer Information Science faculty at
Washtenaw Community College, Ann Arbor, MI

Why Python?

In a world of ever-increasing scripting and language platforms, why choose Python, a legacy system that has been in development on-and-off for nearly two dozen years? Quite simply, it provides a design philosophy that emphasizes code readability without sacrificing a compact and powerful expression of ideas. Going back as far as 1959 with the introduction of COBOL, people have been trying to produce a programming system that is readable, which is to say it does not lend itself to obscuring details or requiring intense concentration to figure out the meaning of a line of code. As any student of computer science can tell you, the problem with COBOL was it couldn't get out of its own way—it went too far down the path of simplicity and its lack of easy-to-use data structures hurt it the most. The remainder of third-generation languages, such as C, C++, Pascal, and I would even argue Java, were marred by the lack of a concise and powerful string handling system as well as tedious ways to manage collections (lists, dictionaries, sets, and so on).

It cannot be over-emphasized how important basic string handling is in developing modern programs that interface with the textual world of the web, especially unstyled documents (i.e. plain text). Simple things such as concatenation, regular expressions, and splitting and joining strings must be effortless or else they become onerous. Such was the appeal of Perl for many years. In fact, many people will speak of Perl-and-Python in a single breath since they so often occupy the same solution-space. However, the two languages diverge on a few key principles. Specifically, in Perl there are many ways to perform even the simplest operations due to its many operators and ability to nest them in ever-more-complex expressions. In Python, there is generally one way to do something, which means it is both easy to understand and manipulate.

Why harp on readability? Because in the past three decades, research has pointed out that the biggest piece of the pie in most information technology projects is not hardware but people time. Specifically, the productivity of developers sets the cost of implementation, even in many cloud-based apps that employ hundreds of servers. In cases where human activity doesn't beat hardware costs, the costs of getting-to-market faster and, hence, collecting revenue argues for readability. Programmers who can read the code that they and others are writing produce a more reliable product in less time than otherwise.

Why One Hour?

It sounds ludicrous on the face of it: learn a new programming language in just an hour! I agree it is provocative, but its point is that any developer who is proficient in a few languages already, maybe Javascript and C++ for example, can pick up the basics in about an hour. Does that mean that Python is inherently a simple platform? Perhaps it is and perhaps it isn't, but it is simple to learn, beyond a doubt. In terms of expressiveness, it reads a lot like pseudo-code, which is how people write algorithms in English before coding them. With Python, I feel as if I can instantly gain an understanding of code that someone has written in my first reading of it, which is something no one ever said about Perl.

In Java and C++, the program is no longer driven by logic but by an attempt to express relationships through classes. Hence the rise of many diagramming techniques in the past twenty years, including UML, where you are admonished to design fully before the first line of code is written. In this one-hour approach, I will even demonstrate how you can easily re-factor from script to procedural (function-based) to object-oriented without losing your train of thought and without getting mired in analysis-paralysis.

Lastly, I promise not to mire you down in details: we won't look at every method in the string() class or exhaustively plod through the math library. Instead, my goal is to show you the shortest path to achieving success in your own applications.

Where to Get Python?

If you have a Linux distro, you may already have Python installed. In a window, type `python -V` to get the version number. This book is based on Python 3.x. You can use your usual Linux package install tool to upgrade or obtain Python 3.x.

If you have Mac or Windows, there are reputable packages available from:

- www.python.org/downloads/
- www.activestate.com/activepython/downloads
- www.cygwin.com/install.html (part of their Linux-on-Windows suite)

Tablet users: check your local appstore (iTunes or Google Play)

I used the IDLE developer tool to write these examples, but either Notepad++ or Vim make excellent Python development tools.

Lessons Overview and Goals:

1. **Opening and using files (ex1.py)**
   exercise: read in a text file and echo it out (interactive mode)

2. **Change it to a word counting program (ex2.py)**
   exercise: use split(), compute total, write amount at end

3. **Planning for unplanned events: (ex3.py)**
   exercise: add exception handling for opening file

4. **Word frequency counter: (ex4.py)**
   exercise: use collections.Counter to track the words

5. **Subdivide into functions: (ex5.py)**
   exercise: bust out the opening, reading, and printing operations into functions

6. **A dictionary of lists with defaultdict: (ex6.py)**
   exercise: use collections.defaultdict to build an "index" of the file by recording each occurrence of a word in a given line into a list

7. **Constructing a class: (ex7.py)**
   exercise: change a set of functions into a containing class

8. **Understanding Regular Expressions (ex8.py)**
   exercise: phone number pattern matching

9. **Exploring the world of REST APIs (ex9.py)**
   exercise: pull live weather data reports

10. **Using threads for concurrent REST requests (ex10.py)**
    exercise: expand previous weather reports to run on multiple threads

11. **CGI-BIN web programming basics (weather.py)**
    exercise: present an HTML form and display live weather forecast

12. **Implement your own REST server (rest.py)**
    exercise: make the functions from lessons 2 and 5 callable as URLs

Source code for these files is available on http://www.volkman.org/python/

However, consider that you learn more from mistakes than from success, so please try taking the time to type in the exercises on your own. You will learn things.

Preface to the 2nd Edition

The first edition grew organically out of in-house trainings that I had conducted for a brownbag lunch series. The implicit challenge was to deliver some kind of meaningful language overview to those with some prior programming experience, but no exposure to Python itself. In the summer of 2014, I delivered it to an audience of professional developers at a regional "Dev Day" conference in Detroit. At that point, I felt finished with it and basically put it on the shelf.

By late 2016, it was clear that *Learn Python in One Hour* had achieved widespread adoption as an inexpensive eBook introduction in use by several institutions. I knew that more could be done with the subject, but I faced a seemingly overwhelming number of choices. Eventually, I settled on exploring various libraries that most developers would need: regular expressions (re), calling REST APIs (requests), threading, CGI-BIN web programming (cgi and cgitb), and implementing your REST server (web.py).

To motivate these more advanced topics, a suitable problem set was needed. Specifically, something that could express the difficult concepts in the fewest number of lines of code. At that point, I stumbled on the idea of a threaded weather forecast retriever and everything slipped into place in an hour... roughly!

Lesson One – Opening Arguments

One of my mid-career mentors, Ralph Almer, once said to me: "When you break it down, most computing boils down to: read a file, do some processing, and write out another file." In this vein, we shall begin at the beginning; our first program will open a file, echo it out, and close the file handle. It seems simple enough, and this sort of benchmark "Hello World" is often used as a crude benchmark to assess the difficulty of learning a programming platform. In my experience, this is absolutely true considering the arcane preambles required in environments such as COBOL or Java just to get to the point where you can "do something" with input data. For our first attempt, we'll do the following:

```
1:   # Exercise 1: opening and using a file
2:
3:   fh = open("c:/temp/input.txt", "r", encoding="ascii")
4:   for line in fh:
5:       print("read: %s" % line)
6:   fh.close()
```

This exercise may seem like a lot of gibberish or "not too bad" depending on your comfort level with programming syntaxes. Yes, we're ignoring error handling on purpose here; I have to save something for Lesson Two! Let's break it down: line #1 says we're to open a file with an MS-DOS path as shown. If you prefer old-school backslashes (e.g. "c:\temp"), you'll have to double them up. As in C++, the backslash is an escape character that allows you to enter characters that are difficult or impossible to represent readably. So if you insist on MS-DOS paths, then substitute open("C:\\tmp\\input.txt").

The next two arguments specify the mode "r" is "read," as all C programmers will remember. The third argument shows how optional parameters can be specified. This means we can cherry-pick the arguments we want to use and ignore the rest. We won't cover open() in great detail here; you can find meticulous detail on docs.python.org.

The *for* loop looks a lot like *for* loops you've seen in most other programming languages. The difference here is that our variable called *fh* is an iterator that allows you to traverse its contents on a line-oriented basis. Where "line" means whatever is natural for the OS where you are running the program. Of course, there are byte and block-oriented ways to read and write files, but we're limiting ourselves to text processing for the course of our one-hour lesson on Python.

Last, but not least, we close the file handle to avoid leaking resources. This step is not just good hygiene but actually functional because many operating systems do not allow open files to be moved or deleted.

Please note the use of indenting to show program "blocks" instead of some type of correctly (or incorrectly) placed braces { }. The block indent is part of the self-documenting feature of Python so there is never a doubt what nesting level you are in. The trailing colon ":" at the end of line #4 clues us in that a block-indent is required ahead.

Here's the input file we'll use:

```
now is the time
for all good people
to come to the aid of their country
etc etc etc etc
```

So when we run the program, we get:

```
read: now is the time

read: for all good people

read: to come to the aid of their country

read: etc etc etc etc
```

Well, that's interesting.... Why do we get double-spaced output? The reason is that the *newline* which marks the end of the line, gets reproduced exactly into the line buffer. That would be fine except print() assumes that everything handed to it would like to have a newline added. If you want to continue to use print(), the least painful way is to add an additional optional parameter, *end* = "" which means "add nothing to what I say to print."

```
5:      print("read: %s" % line, end="")
```

Lesson Two – Using Your Words

After reading a file, the next logical thing to do is to analyze its contents. In this demo, we're just going to count the total number of words in an ASCII plain text file. A "word" is any run of printable characters delimited by blanks either before or after it. In each new code example, we'll highlight the new code in boldface so you don't need to remember the previous lesson or flip back-and-forth trying to guess what's different.

```
 1:  #Exercise #2: counting words in a file
 2:
 3:  fh = open("c:/temp/input.txt", "r", encoding="ascii")
 4:  numWords = 0
 5:  for line in fh:
 6:      words = line.split()
 7:      numWords = numWords + len(words)
 8:
 9:  print ("I got %d words" % numWords)
10:  fh.close()
```

In line #5, we introduce numWords by assignment, and you will notice that no "declaration" was required. This is typical of scripting languages and will be familiar to Perl or Bash developers. Although we assigned numWords an integer value now, that doesn't mean that numWords must be forever bound to that type of data. You may wish to think of the *type* as an attribute of the data itself.

In line #6, we're dynamically creating a list-type through the use of the split() method on a string. You can split on any set of delimiters, but we'll just take the default space (" ") as it serves the purpose. In the following len, we accumulate the total by adding in the length of the list. Because you can index a list by square-brackets and an index, e.g. words[3], you're welcome to consider a list to be a traditional array type container.

Although you'll probably develop your own style of Python coding, my personal preference is to leave a blank line at the end of a block (as in line #8). I find it helps me visually match my attention to a particular area of the program as I develop and debug it further. When we run it, we just get the summary:

```
I got 20 words
```

Lesson Three – When Things Go Wrong

Inevitably, all applications have file I/O problems: either we run out of space writing a file, files go missing, permissions are broken, and the list goes on. The way we handle unhappy events in Python is with the try/except/finally block. Let's take a first hack at it:

```
 1:  # Exercise #3a: exception handling - first try
 2:
 3:  try:
 4:      fh = open("c:/temp/XXXinput.txt", "r", encoding="ascii")
 5:  except OSError as e:
 6:      print("error %d reading file %s" % (e.errno, e.filename ) )
 7:      quit()
 8:
 9:  numWords = 0
10:  for line in fh:
11:      words = line.split()
12:      numWords += len(words)
13:  fh.close()
14:
15:  print("I got %d words" % numWords))
```

What's new this time around is, of course, lines #3–7, which attempt to get us out of the program as gracefully as possible. You can imagine in a much larger program it might try for an alternate filename, re-prompt the user, etc. Another method to end in the middle of a program would be sys.exit().

This version is a little overly-optimistic because, in theory, maybe our file is on a network drive and the network gets flaky during the read loop, etc. Also it belies my previous life as a C++ programmer and is less than Pythonic. A more pristine approach is shown in Exercise 3B on the next page.

```
# Exercise #3b: exception handling - context-manager "with"

numWords = 0
try:
    with open("c:/temp/input.txt", "r", encoding="ascii") as fh:
        for line in fh:
            words = line.split()
            numWords += len(words)
except OSError as e:
    print("error %d reading file %s" % (e.errno, e.filename ) )

print("I got %d words" % numWords)
```

The *with* statement introduces a block of code that works with an object using a context-manager. As such, the whole lifetime of the file is encapsulated in the with-block. The unseen magic here is that the file object's destructor is called at the end and closes the file automatically so you'll notice there's no fh.close() at all. As an added bonus, we get OSErrors handled correctly for all phases: opening, reading, and closing the file.

The try-except block has a third component called "finally" whereby we can do a closing-type action regardless of whether or not we had an exception. There's more to it, but it's beyond the scope of our one-hour lesson.

Lesson Four – What's the Frequency, Kenneth?

In Lesson Four, we're going to start tracking the frequency of each word in the input file. For the sake of simplicity, we'll use the first type of exception handling and not take advantage of the more robust *with* context-manager. Differences from Exercise #3 are highlighted by boldface:

```
 1:  # Exercise #4: word frequency counter
 2:
 3:  import collections
 4:
 5:  try:
 6:      fh = open("c:/temp/input.txt", "r", encoding="ascii")
 7:  except OSError as e:
 8:      print("error %d reading file %s" % (e.errno, e.filename ) )
 9:      quit()
10:
11:  numWords = 0
12:  wordFreq = collections.Counter()
13:  for line in fh:
14:      words = line.split()
15:      numWords += len(words)
16:      for word in words:
17:          wordFreq[word] += 1
18:  fh.close()
19:
20:  print("I got %d words" % numWords)
21:  for key in sorted(wordFreq.keys() ):
22:      print("key %-12s found %2d times" % (key, wordFreq[key]) )
```

The import statement brings in different canned libraries, either system or user, for use with the current program. By default, a library's namespace comes in directly and you can locate members with the dot "." operator, such as in line #12 *collections.Counter()*. The collections library is, of course, a system library, but you still need to import it. This process is very familiar to C++ programmers who would use *#include* or in Java they would use *package*.

The *Counter* collection object (line #12) allows you to create a dictionary (or "hash") that maps keys to values. The advantage of counter is you don't have to initialize the count of each object to zero, as you would with Python's built-in *dict* object. Moving on to lines #16-17, we nest another *for* loop to iterate the words array one word at a time. Then we just increment wordFreq's counter indexed by the word element.

Lastly, in lines #21-22, we'll traverse the wordFreq collection in sorted order by sorting the keys that we use to access it. After all, a dictionary is just a collection of key/value pairs so we can extract the keys and sort them in one step. The output is then sorted by word:

```
I got 20 words
key aid           found  1 times
key all           found  1 times
key come          found  1 times
key country       found  1 times
key etc           found  4 times
key for           found  1 times
key good          found  1 times
key is            found  1 times
key now           found  1 times
key of            found  1 times
key people        found  1 times
key the           found  2 times
key their         found  1 times
key time          found  1 times
key to            found  2 times
>>>
```

You might well say, "This isn't what I wanted: I wanted it to sort by word frequency, not the words themselves!" The sorted() method can be tasked to that as well; the difference is that you redefine the key as the value with the argument key=wordFreq.get as shown below:

```
23: print("Order by frequency descending")
24: for key in sorted(wordFreq, key=wordFreq.get, reverse=True):
25:     print("key %-12s found %2d times" % (key, wordFreq[key]) )
```

Which yields the expected result:

```
Order by frequency descending
key etc           found  4 times
key the           found  2 times
key to            found  2 times
key come          found  1 times
key all           found  1 times
     ... and so on ...
```

Lesson Five – Fun with Functions

At this point, we're starting to approach the limit of what you want to do in a script. We might start tacking on more complexity, such as deeper nesting or simply more and more code, but doing so begins reversing course on our goals of readability to say nothing of maintainability. The basic unit of work in a program should be a function, which is literally the same as a basic algebra function like $f(x,y) = 2x + y2$. The point is that the function is fully parameterized in that the output depends only on the input. The main extra benefits are, of course: ease of testing and ability to divvy up work between team members. We'll take a simpleton's way out for partitioning the code into three functions. This isn't a course on how to best modularize your code, but modularize we will:

```
 1:  # Exercise #5: busting out functions
 2:
 3:  import collections
 4:
 5:  def openFile():
 6:      fh = None
 7:      try:
 8:          fh = open("c:/temp/input.txt", "r", encoding="ascii")
 9:      except OSError as e:
10:          print("error %d reading file %s" % (e.errno, e.filename) )
11:          quit()
12:      return fh
13:
14:  def processFile(fh):
15:      numWords = 0
16:      wordFreq = collections.Counter()
17:      for line in fh:
18:          words = line.split()
19:          numWords += len(words)
20:          for word in words:
21:              wordFreq[word] += 1
22:      fh.close()
23:      return numWords, wordFreq
24:
25:  def printReport(numWords: int, wordFreq: dict):
26:      print("I got %d words" % numWords)
27:      for key in sorted(wordFreq.keys() ):
28:          print("key %-12s found %2d times" % (key, wordFreq[key]) )
29:
30:  def main():
```

```
31:        fh = openFile()
32:        (nw, wf) = processFile(fh)
33:        printReport(nw, wf)
34:
35: if __name__ == "__main__":
36:      main()
```

Our purpose is to subdivide the tasks of the program into three sequential groups of code that use parameters to communicate essential information with each other. This "locality" of information helps make debugging easier because it hides details that a function doesn't need to know. For example, printReports() need not concern itself with file handles at all. That being said, it's a pretty arbitrary division of labor, and most people might reduce it to two functions, but we're using three here to give more flavor without adding new ingredients to the code.

Converting the code into functions is relatively easy in a Python-friendly editor, such as IDLE, which allows you to highlight and tab-in a selection in a few seconds. Manually adjusting the spacing is a way to introduce logic errors into your code, unless you are extremely careful.

Each function block begins with *def* for "defining" the function and a full list of parameters. By default, you have read-only access to global variables inside your function. If you must modify a global variable, then a special *global* keyword must appear inside your function to declare your intent to do mayhem. In Python, parameters are passed by assignment. If you pass in a mutable object such as an array or dictionary, then, of course, the function can modify it. In general, because multiple return values are so easy to use in Python, as shown in line #23, there's no need to create an artificial "return object" like you would in Java.

Lastly, you see the newly minted main() function in lines #30–33. Because Python is an interpreter, it is actually interpreting lines sequentially throughout the program. There is no magic main() function like you see in C++ or Java; I could have called it macaroni() if I wanted to. Up until line #35, the whole program is a series of declarations of functions, and without the explicit invocation of main() on line #36, the program exits without doing anything.

The *if* __name__ statement is asking the interpreter whether we are the primary target of Python. For example, in an included library, this test would fail to execute main(). This is one way to establish unit-testing for Python programs. Each library module can be tested by invoking Python standalone, and it can run its various test stubs accordingly. Python uses a path-based approach to locate libraries, similar in to how Java locates them, but without the "dotted" hierarchy management.

Lesson Six – A Dictionary of Lists

We've developed our word frequency count as far as it's going to go, so the next type of analysis we'll add is that of an "index." By index, I mean the type of reference you find in the back of an old-fashioned paper book, which shows each word and the number of the page on which it appears. In our case, we'll show each word and the line number it appears on:

```
 1:   # Exercise #6: dictionary of lists
 2:
 3:   import collections
 4:
 5:   def openFile():
 6:       fh = None
 7:       try:
 8:           fh = open("c:/temp/input.txt", "r", encoding="ascii")
 9:       except OSError as e:
10:           print("error %d reading file %s" % (e.errno, e.filename) )
11:           quit()
12:       return fh
13:
14:   def processFile(fh):
15:       numWords = 0
16:       wordFreq = collections.Counter()
17:       wordIndex = collections.defaultdict(list)
18:       lineNum = 0
19:       for line in fh:
20:           lineNum += 1
21:           words = line.split()
22:           numWords += len(words)
23:           for word in words:
24:               wordFreq[word] += 1
25:               wordIndex[word].append(str(lineNum))
26:       fh.close()
27:       return (numWords, wordFreq, wordIndex)
28:
29:   def printReport(stats: tuple):
30:       (numWords, wordFreq, wordIndex) = stats
31:       print("I got %d words" % numWords)
32:       for key in sorted(wordFreq.keys() ):
33:           print("key %-12s found %2d times" % (key, wordFreq[key]) )
34:       for key in sorted(wordIndex.keys() ):
35:           print("key %-12s found on lines: %s" % (key,
36:                   ",".join(wordIndex[key] ) ) )
```

```
37:
38:  def main():
39:      fh = openFile()
40:      stats = processFile(fh)
41:      printReport(stats)
42:
43:  if __name__ == "__main__":
44:      main()
```

Okay, this code is getting kind of long, so we'll simply focus in on the boldfaced code, which is new since the previous lesson. On line #17, we create wordIndex as a *defaultdict* where each entry is a *list*. Although we have never previously declared the data types of what's inside a container, doing so is necessary to harness the power of *defaultdict*. Those of you familiar with Java and C++ are used to having to script out elaborate declarations of every type of data structure in advance. Normally with a Python dictionary, you need to test for the presence of an entry before you can increment or append an item. With *defaultdict*, you get a blank entry automatically generated of the type you specified (*list* in this case). Specifically, an empty list *[ ]* in this case. Technically, *list* is a factory function that supplies missing values.

On line #25, we're appending the current line number in the file to the value in wordIndex which is specified by the value of *word*.

On lines #35-36, we're dumping out the content of the list of lines as a comma-separated list via the *join()* string method. This is a handy way to produce any value-separated string from a list of strings. Because it only works on strings, we had to cast the numbers to strings back on line #25 as shown below:

```
25:                    wordIndex[word].append(str(lineNum))
```

Also on lines #35-36, notice that we have split the code between two lines. Normally Python requires an entire statement to fit on one line. Because we had a "live" open parenthesis on line #35, we can carry over to line #36 and keep typing. In cases where you can't continue a parenthesized expression, you can end the line with a backslash "\" which says, "Wait; I'm not done yet." Python etiquette argues against very long lines of text. This is one principle of "Pythonic" programming. There are other principles, but most require knowledge outside the scope of this brief introduction.

Next, let's look at the output with an eye to how we could make it more useful:

```
key aid          found on lines: 3
key all          found on lines: 2
key come         found on lines: 3
key country      found on lines: 3
key etc          found on lines: 4,4,4,4
    :
    .
key the          found on lines: 1,3
key their        found on lines: 3
key time         found on lines: 1
key to           found on lines: 3,3
```

Normally, you wouldn't want repeating values in any type of index. Especially in the index of a book, for example. We can mitigate this problem by changing our containers in the dictionary from list to set. By definition, a set contains one and only one instance of an item, so problem solved:

```
14:  def processFile(fh):
15:      numWords = 0
16:      wordFreq = collections.Counter()
17:      wordIndex = collections.defaultdict(set)
18:      lineNum = 0
19:      for line in fh:
20:          lineNum += 1
21:          words = line.split()
22:          numWords += len(words)
23:          for word in words:
24:              wordFreq[word] += 1
25:              wordIndex[word].add(str(lineNum))
26:      fh.close()
27:      return (numWords, wordFreq, wordIndex)
```

Yields this output:

```
key aid          found on lines: 3
key all          found on lines: 2
key come         found on lines: 3
key country      found on lines: 3
key etc          found on lines: 4
    :
    .
key the          found on lines: 1,3
key their        found on lines: 3
key time         found on lines: 1
key to           found on lines: 3
```

On line #17, we changed it from a dictionary of lists to a dictionary of sets.

On line #15, we use the set-specific method add() rather than the list-specific method append().

In general, you'll see that a lot of operations apply to more than one type of container. For example, you can take the length of a set, a dictionary, or a list all by saying `len(x)`. However, you would be mistaken if you think that all these collections are derived from a base class. Instead, what you're seeing is called *duck typing*. The principle is simple: if it walks like a duck, quacks like a duck, and flies like a duck, it probably is a duck. Duck typing gives you polymorphism without inheritance. In other words, all the good parts without the bad parts. It also means that a well-written program could accept a list or a set as a function parameter. You can inquire the type of an expression with `type(x)`. This is much farther afield than we will go in our one-hour lesson.

Lesson Seven – A Touch of Class

There comes a time in the evolution of any script when you've exceeded the recommended complexity for procedural (function-based) programming. Side effects of this situation may include ever-growing parameter lists, lost time spent hunting down the right function, diminished productivity, nausea, or dizziness. We won't give you a dramatic cure in our one-hour lesson, but just a small dose so you can see the basic idea of class definitions. In an effort to keep it simple, we will use a rather poor class design that no one would recommend. The point is to build the simplest class-wrapper that we can around our three pet functions. As you might have guessed, object-oriented design methodology is outside the scope of our one-hour lesson. Many of the basic ideas from C++ or Java apply, except for the distinctions of *public*, *private*, and *protected*.

```
 1:   # Exercise #7: class wrapping
 2:
 3:   import collections
 4:
 5:   class docIndexer:
 6:       def __init__(self):
 7:           pass
 8:
 9:       def openFile(self, filename):
10:           self.fh = None
11:           try:
12:               self.fh = open(filename, "r", encoding="ascii")
13:           except OSError as e:
14:               print("error %d reading file" % e.errno )
15:               return False
16:           return True
17:
18:       def processFile(self):
19:           numWords = 0
20:           wordFreq = collections.Counter()
21:           wordIndex = collections.defaultdict(set)
22:           lineNum = 0
23:           for line in self.fh:
24:               lineNum += 1
25:               words = line.split()
26:               numWords += len(words)
27:               for word in words:
28:                   wordFreq[word] += 1
```

```
29:                          wordIndex[word].add(str(lineNum))
30:              self.fh.close()
31:              self.stats = (numWords, wordFreq, wordIndex)
32:
33:          def printReport(self):
34:              (numWords, wordFreq, wordIndex) = self.stats
35:              print("I got %d words" % numWords)
36:              for key in sorted(wordFreq.keys() ):
37:                  print("key %-12s found %2d " % (key, wordFreq[key]) )
38:              for key in sorted(wordIndex.keys() ):
39:                  print("key %-12s found on lines: %s" % (key,
40:                          ",".join(wordIndex[key] ) ) )
41:
42:  def main():
43:      di = docIndexer()
44:      if di.openFile("c:/temp/input.txt"):
45:          di.processFile()
46:          di.printReport()
47:
48:  if __name__ == "__main__":
49:      main()
```

Again, I feel impelled to say that the point of this class design was simply to show how code can be promoted from procedural (function-oriented) to object-oriented with far less pain than C++, and, in fact, procedural code isn't even a design choice in Java. Each of our functions has been "tabbed right" and is subsumed under the new class docIndexer as declared on line #5. Each non-static method has a *self* local variable that points to the object and stands-in for *this* in C++ or Java. Static methods are outside the scope of our one-hour lesson.

The constructor __*init*__ shown in lines #6-7 is optional and only for show in this class. You will also notice the new pass statement, which is a do-nothing (NOP) placeholder required if you declare a block. The preceding line #6 ends with a colon ":" so a block is declared so a statement must follow or else a compile error occurs. Following the advice of C++ guru Scott Meyers, who admonishes that "constructors should never fail," I endeavor to keep them simple, and therefore, I do not even try to open a file inside a constructor.

Jumping down to the main() function once more (lines #43-46), we have stored a reference to the docIndexer() object in *di* and then used it to address the methods. You will notice that no other return values are used to communicate between *processFile()* and *printReport()*. Where did numWords, wordFreq, and wordIndex go? Yes, we've stuffed them into the object because they naturally relate to both methods (see lines #31 and #34). Rather than carve out one space for each of the three items,

I've chosen to encapsulate them in a single container called a "tuple" titled *stats*. Thanks to duck-typing, tuples act more-or-less like an ad-hoc list; you can pass them, return them, or embed them in a list, dictionary, or whatever. For example, you can use an index de-reference square brackets [n] to pull out the nth element, just like with a list.

In Python, you generally draw the line by declaring a value to be internal with a polite convention of beginning it with a leading underscore. However, there are no draconian enforcers to prevent you from accessing values. In the modern world, we generally use class methods rather than intentionally exposing class data members. In Python, we don't slavishly write setters and getters; techniques called *descriptors* and *properties* can achieve this effect.

In "Hour Two", we'll look beyond Python syntax and venture into it's application libraries and techniques you'll want to use to solve real-world problems.

Lesson Eight – Keeping it Regular

A regular expression (hereafter just "regex") is a mini programming language which simply describes search patterns that can be used to find and even replace a "string within a string". You've already used at least some primitive regexes if you've ever used, for example, Windows Explorer to locate all the xml files on your c: drive ("*.xml") or a Linux command shell to do the same thing: `find . -name *.xml`. The asterisk (*) and question mark (?) are primitive regexes used in finding files in filesystems. The asterisk means "match zero or more characters" and question mark means "match a single character" In this case, the strings that they are searching is the set of all filenames on your computer or subset of folders you specified.

The ability to easily use regexes to solve searches in text files is a hallmark of effective scripting languages such as Python and Perl. To begin, we'll always need to import Python's regular expression library, known as just "re". Let's just throw out a problem to motivate us, we have a line of text and we want to count up all the occurrences of the word "to". Speaking in more general terms, we'll call this sample string a *token*. The string is below:

```
"To be (or not to) be a tool."
```

You can see right off the bat there are several challenges: we need to be case-insensitive ("To" counts the same as "to"), we have punctuation such as parenthesis butting up against the token, and in one case the token is a substring of another word ("to" is part of the word "tool").

As part of this investigation, we're going to get you comfortable with the Read Evaluate Print Loop (REPL) – the interactive shell that Python provides. It is just the right solution for testing ad-hoc code, which is usually the fastest way to test out the usefulness of a given regex. To get there, you simply launch Python without specifying a Python program filename:

```
$ python3

>>> import re
>>> str = "To tattoo (or not to) a tool"
>>> pat = re.compile("to", re.IGNORECASE)
>>> pat.findall(str)
['To', 'to', 'to', 'to']
```

So we've solved two out of three criteria with this simple two-character regular expression ("to"): it matches all permutations of mixed-case including "TO", "to", "To" and "tO", and it works around punctuation such as "to)". Unfortunately, it found twice as many copies of the token by looking inside *tattoo* and *tool*:

    "**To** ta**too** (or not **to**) a **too**l"
      1   2   3   4

Compare this with a brute-force approach of using split(), which is the only tool we had up until now! Isolating all the "to" tokens while ignoring when they appear inside other words would be a really hard problem except for a special character sequence "\b" which does this:

> \b Matches the *empty string*, but only at the beginning or end of a word. A word is defined as a sequence of alphanumeric or underscore characters, so the end of a word is indicated by whitespace or a non-alphanumeric, non-underscore character.

Here's a short program which marches through all these

```
 1:# Exercise #8: case-insensitive search in regular expression
 2: import re
 3: regex = r"\bto\b"
 4: test_str = "To be (or not to) be a tool."
 5: matches = re.finditer(regex, test_str, re.IGNORECASE)
 6:
 7: for matchNum, match in enumerate(matches):
 8:     matchNum = matchNum + 1
 9:     print ("Match %s was found at %d-%d: %s" % (
10:             matchNum, match.start(), match.end(), match.group()))
```

Which yields this output:

```
Match 1 was found at 0-2: To
Match 2 was found at 14-16: to
```

Thus far, we've looked at using regex to search a string for substrings and count up the matches. More common use cases involve extracting unknown strings that fit a well-defined pattern in the source. This also provides the side-effect of validating a pattern vs. an input string.   The most common of these are USA phone number and USA Social Security number. We'll try simple USA phone number with explicit "area code":

> 111-222-3333

The first set of digits is the "area code" (111), the second is the "exchange" (222), and the third block is the "telephone number" (333). The easiest way to write the regex might be: \d{3}-\d{3}-\d{4}

- The \d is another special character sequence that represents "exactly one digit in the range from zero to nine"

- The {3} represents three repetitions of the previous item.

- The dash "-" standing on its own, is simply matched with a dash on the input. There are other uses for dash , but we won't get into them in this lesson

Now, there are plenty of great tools other than Python for you to start experimenting with. One I recommend is called www.regex101.com which lets you type the regex and sample input to show you how well your regex is (or isn't) working. A wise man once said, "Finding strings is one problem. When you decide to use regexes, now you have two problems". What this means is, a regex often needs debugging just like any other type of code, since it is a mini-program within your program.

While the pattern above is good enough to recognize a valid number, we want to also extract the number so we can store it efficiently without hyphens in our database. To do this, we'll add *groups* into the mix. Groups are simply parentheses which delimit your pattern into smaller useful pieces

> (\d{3})-(\d{3})-(\d{4})

```
python3
Python 3.3.5 (default, Jun 17 2014, 12:33:56)
>>> import re
>>> tel_pat = re.compile(r'(\d{3})-(\d{3})-(\d{4})')
>>> my_num = "800-555-1212"
>>> match = tel_pat.match(my_num)
>>> if match:
...     print("Area code %s, exchange %s, number %s" % (match.group(1),
match.group(2), match.group(3)))
Area code 800, exchange 555, number 1212
```

Remember not to type in the ">>>" and "..." if you are typing this in at home. Those are just feedback from the Python REPL system. The next thing to try on your own is `re.sub()` which lets you do find-and-replace operations.

Lesson Nine – Taking a REST

In the bad old days, programmers would hack together "screen scrapers" to program-matically download and translate onscreen data so that some other application could use it. In other words, taking what you can and do see on your web browser and manipulating it like raw data. Nowadays, that is considered unfriendly behavior and can lead to getting your IP address blacklisted! Fortunately, most major online services have an API (Applications Programming Interface) that allows you to legally access their data under terms and conditions that you agree to when registering for an "API Key". The Key uniquely identifies your account so your compliance can be metered. The overarching approach is called Representational State Transfer (REST) for short.

In this exercise, you'll register for an API Key from OpenWeatherMap and write a program to display data about your current weather conditions. To get started, register for your unique key online at https://openweathermap.org/price and be sure to choose the "free" option.

But we're getting ahead of ourselves here, first we need to know how to fetch web pages using Python. The best choice is Kenneth Reitz' requests library (http://docs.python-requests.org) . Python 2.x used a library called urllib2 for HTTP which was later split into urllib.request and urllib.error. However, requests library has a much nicer API so use "pip3 install requests" to bring in that one as well.

The first thing you may run into is needing to install requests on your computer. Since this is a 3rd party library, we'll probably have to either put it in ourselves or find a system administrator to do that for us. Pip3 is the recursive (self-referential) acronym for "Pip Installs Python' or "PIP Installs Packages". With pip3, you can install, remove, upgrade, and otherwise modify any and all 3rd party libraries.

```
$ sudo pip3 install requests
pip3 install requests
Collecting requests
  Downloading requests-2.18.4-py2.py3-none-any.whl (88kB)
    100% |                                    | 92kB 3.5MB/s
Installing collected packages: urllib3, certifi, idna, chardet, requests
Successfully installed certifi-2017.7.27.1 chardet-3.0.4 idna-2.6
requests-2.18.4 urllib
```

```
```

Now you will be able to do the necessary imports, in this case "import requests"

Once you've gotten your free API key back, we can try out the API call. You can either paste this into your webbrowser or use the Linux commandline tool curl to see it. Be sure to use your own API key, not mine!

```
$ curl
"http://api.openweathermap.org/data/2.5/weather?q=London,uk&appid=f4aa63
05ea8940b3f24bb23c6b0fe4c3"

{"coord":{"lon":-
0.13,"lat":51.51},"weather":[{"id":521,"main":"Rain","description":"shower
rain","icon":"09d"}],"base":"stations","main":{"temp":287.59,"pressure":1012
,"humidity":51,"temp_min":284.15,"temp_max":289.15},"visibility":10000,"wind
":{"speed":2.6},"clouds":{"all":40},"dt":1505485200,"sys":{"type":1,"id":509
1,"message":0.0045,"country":"GB","sunrise":1505453792,"sunset":1505499200},
"id":2643743,"name":"London","cod":200}
```

So we get a strangely organized bunch of information about the weather in London. This nesting of data structures is a system called JSON, an open standard for describing hierarchical data (JavaScript Object Notation). You may want to try cutting-and-pasting the JSON output displayed above to www.jsonprettyprint.com. This is a free service which converts a JSON string to a nested display of containers (usually dictionaries and arrays). If your Python system doesn't include the json import library, use pip3 to install that as well.

Take a moment now to review the Open Weather Map API documentation for "current" weather at http://openweathermap.org/current. We see several things of importance:

- The base url is http://api.openweathermap.org/data/2.5/ this means it conforms to version 2.5 of their published API.

- The path for this particular request is weather, which we will append to the base URL, giving http://api.openweathermap.org/data/2.5/weather

```
import requests

url = "http://api.openweathermap.org/data/2.5/weather"
params = {"q" : "London,uk" , "units" : "imperial" , "appid":
"f4aa6305ea8940b3f24bb23c6b0fe4c3"}
rq = requests.get(url, params)
print(rq.text)
```

The output should look identical to what you got from curl or your web browser, so we won't repeat it here. Instead, let's do some things to crack open that long tedious JSON string. We'll use json.loads() to turn JSON text into a native Python nested dictionary. Then we can write a humanly readable report to display on a web page.

```
 1: # Exercise #9: Using the OpenWeatherMap REST API
 2: import json
 3: import requests
 4:
 5: url = "http://api.openweathermap.org/data/2.5/weather"
 6: params = {"q" : "London,uk" , "units": "imperial", "appid":
"f4aa6305ea8940b3f24bb23c6b0fe4c3"}
 7: rq = requests.get(url, params)
 8: jd = json.loads(rq.text)
 9: high_temp = float(jd['main']['temp_max'])
10: print("Today's high will be %3.1f degrees F" % high_temp)
11: if high_temp > 80.0:
12:     print("Let's go to the beach!")
13: elif high_temp < 25.0:
14:     print("Let's go skiing!")
```

Gives us ouput like this:

```
    Today's high will be 60.8 degrees F
```

The high temperature is extracted on line #9 by de-referencing a nested dictionary of dictionaries. This could, of course, be done in two steps and you could argue it would be safer not to assume that just because the first lookup jd['main'] works that jd['main']['temp_max'] will always be there. That is an act of faith we have put in our code.

Examining rq.text by pasting the output from the curl command shows usthere is an outer-level dictionary which contains entries: "coord", "weather", "base", "main", "visibility" and so on. The full contents of jd['main'] are:

```
"main": {
    "temp": 287.59,
    "pressure": 1012,
    "humidity": 51,
    "temp_min": 284.15,
    "temp_max": 289.15
  },
```

Lesson Ten - Untangling Threads

By default, Python supports an execution model where multiple threads can be executing on a single CPU core within a program. Note that I have not mentioned a scenario where each thread gets a dedicated CPU. This is available in the multithreading module which is out of scope of this chapter. However, porting your code from the threading module to the multithreading module is easy once you have mastered the basics of threading.

In the basic Python threading module (import threading), the Global Interpreter Lock (GIL) ensures that only one of however many threads you have launched is running. What good is this? Well, it turns out a large number of data processing projects turn out to be "hurry up and wait" scenarios where program execution naturally stalls while waiting for input, a call to external program, or even an HTTP REST call. Why not take advantage of this downtime to allow control to yield to another thread which is not waiting?

In this chapter, we'll adapt the OpenWeatherMap HTTP REST call from Chapter 8 to the threading environment so we can have an arbitrary number of threads querying multiple cities simultaneously. As always, it pays to divide-and-conquer a new problem. Rather than maximizing the amount of code in a given function, the approach is to completely encapsulate blocks of code into functions with easily understandable inputs and outputs. For exercise #10, this will include

- weather_report(url, location): construct a requests object from the base url, predefined parameters, and a single parameter for the geographic location. If you skipped Chapter 8 go back and review it.

- worker(url, input_queue): launched as a thread, it's job is to be a consumer of items on the input_queue and a producer of items on the output_queue. In between, it gets its work done by calling weather_report().

- main(): populates the input_queue, launches the threads, and calmly waits for them to finish. The rendezvous takes place when the queue becomes empty by calling input_queue.join().

```
 1: # Exercise #10: threaded weather report demo
 2: # Adapted from an idea at
https://pymotw.com/2/Queue/index.html#module-Queue
 3: import requests
 4: import json
 5: import threading
 6: import queue  # replaces import Queue in python 2.x
 7:
 8: def weather_report(url: str, location: str):
 9:     params = {"q" : location , "units": "imperial", "appid":
"f4aa6305ea8940b3f24bb23c6b0fe4c3"}
10:     rq = requests.get(url, params)
11:     jd = json.loads(rq.text)
12:     high_temp = float(jd['main']['temp_max'])
13:     low_temp = float(jd['main']['temp_min'])
14:     return location, low_temp, high_temp
15:
16: def worker(url: str, input_queue: queue.Queue(), output_queue:
queue.Queue()):
17:     while not input_queue.empty():
18:         try:
19:             location = input_queue.get(block=True, timeout=1)
20:         except queue.Empty:
21:             return
22:         weather_tuple = weather_report(url, location)
23:         output_queue.put(weather_tuple)
24:         input_queue.task_done()
25:
26: def main():
27:     threads = []
28:     num_threads = 3
29:     url = "http://api.openweathermap.org/data/2.5/weather"
30:     input_queue = queue.Queue()
31:     output_queue = queue.Queue()
32:     for city in ['Detroit', 'London', 'Chicago', 'Miami', 'Prague',
33:                  'Ann Arbor', 'Mackinac Island', 'Hell,MI',
34:                  'Paradise,MI', 'Misery Bay,MI','Bad Axe,MI']:
35:         input_queue.put(city)
36:
37:     for i in range(num_threads):
38:         t = threading.Thread(target=worker, args=(url, input_queue,
output_queue))
39:         threads.append(t)
40:         t.start()
41:
42:     print('*** Main thread waiting')
43:     input_queue.join()
44:     print('*** Done')
45:     while not output_queue.empty():
```

```
46:          (location, low_temp, high_temp) = output_queue.get()
47:          print("%-20s: Low %3.1fF, High %3.1fF" % (location,
low_temp, high_temp))
48:
49: if __name__ == "__main__":
50:     main()
```

Yields this result:

```
*** Main thread waiting
*** Done
Chicago                : Low 86.0F, High 87.8F
London                 : Low 48.2F, High 55.4F
Detroit                : Low 75.2F, High 80.6F
Miami                  : Low 87.8F, High 91.4F
Prague                 : Low 50.0F, High 53.6F
Ann Arbor              : Low 75.2F, High 80.6F
Mackinac Island        : Low 78.8F, High 78.8F
Hell,MI                : Low 77.0F, High 80.6F
Ontanagon,MI           : Low 75.9F, High 75.9F
Misery Bay,MI          : Low 78.8F, High 82.4F
Bad Axe,MI             : Low 69.8F, High 80.6F
```

We'll take a deeper look at some of the code with new concepts, beginning with the worker() function. First let's clear up some terminology. A "queue" is collection type that you can "push" data into and "pop" data out of in an pre-determined order. When customers line up at an ATM cash machine, the first person to join the line will be the first person to get their money out: this is called First-In, First-Out (FIFO for short). The Python queue.Queue() objects are FIFO queues although you can ask for queue.LifoQueue to get a Last-In First-Out behavior analogous to how some playing card games use a discard pile, for example.

The outer-while loop insures that the function runs only as long as there is more work availabe in the input_queue. Now, because of a potential race-condition, we must also check again when we "pop" something from the queue. The thread will pause execution until a queue item is available --or-- one second elapses with no data ("timeout"), whichever comes first. If no data is available within one second, get() fails and queue.Empty Exception must be handled.

```
16: def worker(url: str, input_queue: queue.Queue(), output_queue:
queue.Queue()):
17:     while not input_queue.empty():
18:         try:
19:             location = input_queue.get(block=True, timeout=1)
20:         except queue.Empty:
21:             return
```

I encourage you to run this program several times in a row. Depending on your environment, you'll see that the weather data comes back in a slightly different order from one run to the next. I think that's an important feedback to notice the aysnchronous relationship of thread execution. We're no longer in a deterministic world where the earliest started is always the first to finish.

The worker threads are launched in the main() function:

```
37:      for i in range(num_threads):
38:          t = threading.Thread(target=worker, args=(url, input_queue,
output_queue))
39:          threads.append(t)
40:          t.start()
41:
```

Each pass through the for() loop creates a new thread with the threading.Thread() constructor on line 38. This is the first time we've used functions as objects, but you should notice that by naming worker without a trailing parenthesis, as in worker(), we're acting on a reference or "handle" to a function. The threading library will setup the call to worker() inside the constructor and pass the args as parameters to it. Notice that we are passing a tuple to the args parameter, which allows for any number of arguments to be passed to the target function when it's called. The new thread is teed up, but the starting pistol is not fired until the start() method is called on line 40.

The rendezvous back with the main() thread occurs in line 43 when we invoke join() on the input_queue.

```
42:      print('*** Main thread waiting')
43:      input_queue.join()
44:      print('*** Done')
45:      while not output_queue.empty():
46:          (location, low_temp, high_temp) = output_queue.get()
47:          print("%-20s: Low %3.1fF, High %3.1fF" % (location,
low_temp, high_temp))
```

join() blocks until all items in the queue have been gotten and processed. The count of unfinished tasks goes up whenever an item is added to the queue. The count goes down whenever a consumer thread calls task_done() to indicate that the item was retrieved and all work on it is complete (see line #24). When the count of unfinished tasks drops to zero, join() unblocks.

Lesson Eleven - Spin a Web

Now that we have some expertise in a REST API, we can spin up a webserver and show how Python can serve up HTTP pages including the ever-popular CGI (Common Gateway Interface Binary) standard. CGI was designed in 1993 as a simple way to allow a webserver to execute arbitrary server-side code based on URLs and HTML Forms technologies. It was quickly known as CGI-BIN because the default Unix directory where executable scripts were found was literally named "cgi-bin".

In this chapter, we'll also look at creating your first module—a Python library of functions that exists in another source code file than your main program. Python uses an environment variable called PYTHONPATH to locate modules that may be outside the current directory of execution. We'll skirt the PYTHONPATH in this chapter by locating all of our code (CGI scripts and modules) in the cgi-bin directory.

The goal of our web app is simple: display a form for the user to enter a city name, inquire a forecast from OpenWeather and display it like so:

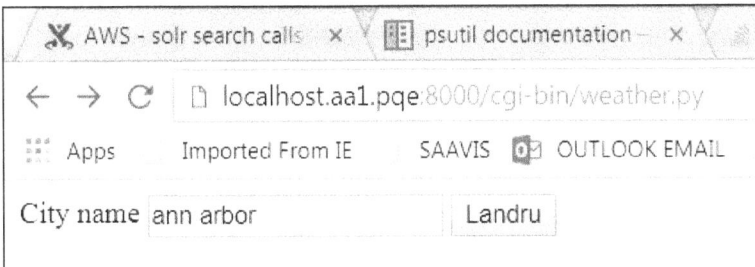

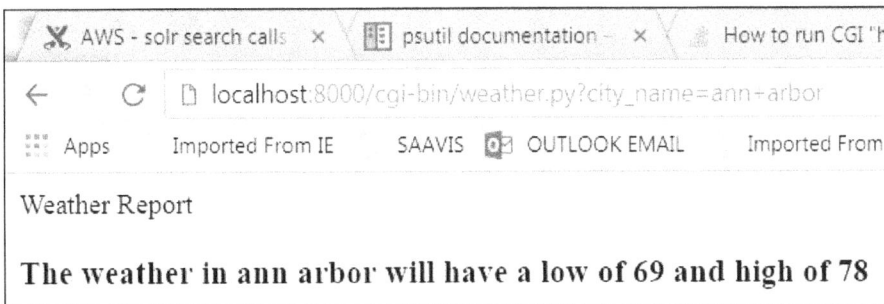

Of course, the first thing we'll need is a friendly HTTP (web) server. Fortunately, Python has a built-in webserver that we run from the computer we're already using. The TCP/IP convention to locate the computer you're using is calling for either

localhost or the IP address it maps to (always 127.0.0.1). It turns out you can use
Python -m to execute any Python module as a script from the commandline:

```
$ python3 -m http.server 8000 --cgi
Serving HTTP on 0.0.0.0 port 8000 ...
172.25.32.74 - - [04/Oct/2017 16:26:47] "GET /cgi-bin/weather.py
HTTP/1.1" 200 -
172.25.32.74 - - [04/Oct/2017 16:26:52] "GET /cgi-
bin/weather.py?city_name=ann+arbor HTTP/1.1" 200 -
```

In this example we run the http.server module at port 8000 and enable CGI-BIN
processing with --cgi. It's important to choose a port number not already in use
because these resources require exclusive access. The HTTP server output shows two
different HTTP GET requests: the first loads weather.py with a blank form and the
second supplies an URL parameter of city_name=ann+arbor. The URI standard does
not allow spaces and reserved puctuation in an URL so the spaces are transformed to
plus signs.

But we're getting ahead of ourselves a little. You've seen that weather.py throws up a
form so now let's look at the source code for weather.py to make that happen:

```
 1: #!/usr/bin/env python3
 2: # Excerise #11:  CGI-BIN with Python (weather.py)
 3: import cgitb
 4: import cgi
 5:
 6: import weather_api
 7:
 8: def main():
 9:     print("Content-Type: text/html; charset=utf-8")   # HTML is
following
10:     print()  # blank line,  end of headers
11:
12:     cgitb.enable()
13:     form = cgi.FieldStorage()
14:     city = form.getvalue("city_name")
15:     if city:
16:         url = "http://api.openweathermap.org/data/2.5/weather"
17:         (location, low_temp, high_temp) =
weather_api.weather_report(url, city)
18:         print("<html><head>Weather Report</head>")
19:         print("<body><h3>The weather in %s will have a low of %d
and high of %d </h3>" % (
20:             location, low_temp, high_temp))
21:         print("</body></html>")
22:     else:
23:         print('<form>City name <input type="text"
name="city_name">')
```

```
24:            print('<input type="submit" value="Landru">')
25:            print('</form action=weather.py>')
26:
27: if __name__ == "__main__":
28:     main()
```

The first thing to notice is new import libaries cgi and cgitb. The cgi library is required to access HTML Forms data (lines 13-14). The cgitb (CGI Trace Back) library solves one of the bigger headaches of CGI programming: the difficulty with reporting Exceptions back to the client. Without line #12, any sort of error would end in mysteriously truncated output returned to the HTTP client.

A typical CGI script is tasked with both displaying and executing a form. You can think of this as a query page and a response page if it makes it easier for you. The determination in line #15 says that if the city_name field has not been filled then we are going to return a query page with a complete HTML Form (lines 23-25) to the web client. If the user does hit the submit button (labelled "Landru") then it will call weather.py again after URL encoding the parameters into the request such that city_name will be filled and we are in a response page mode:

```
http://localhost:8000/cgi-bin/weather.py?city_name=ann+arbor
```

Lines 16-21 demonstrate passing an URL base and the city name to weather_api.weather. First, however, the weather_api.py module has been imported on line #6. All Python modules must end in .py to be considered importable. Furthermore, to satisfy CGI-BIN requirements, they must also be marked as Executable in Unix (use chmod a+x filename.py to do this). Both weather.py and weather_api.py must exist in a cgi-bin folder below where you invoke python3 -m http.server

```
1: #!/usr/bin/env python3
2: #  Excercise #11: weather API module (weather_api.py)
3: import json
4: import requests
5:
6: def weather_report(url: str, location: str):
7:     params = {"q" : location , "units": "imperial", "appid":
"f4aa6305ea8940b3f24bb23c6b0fe4c3"}
8:     rq = requests.get(url, params)
9:     jd = json.loads(rq.text)
10:    high_temp = float(jd['main']['temp_max'])
11:    low_temp = float(jd['main']['temp_min'])
12:    return location, low_temp, high_temp
```

Lesson Twelve - No REST for the wicked

In Lesson Nine, you learned how to make REST API calls on the OpenWeather server. In this lesson, you're going to get to deploy your very own REST server using the web.py framework (www.webpy.org). This framework is specifically designed to allow you to connect up REST responses with the least effort in writing your code. After all, you want to concentrate on the value-add that your code provides, not spend time re-inventing a REST interface.

Our REST server specifically will implement a word count API (/words/count) and a word frequency display API (/words/freq). These functions are lifted from Lessons Two and Five respectively. The word frequency display will use JSON library to send a dictionary back to the web client.

Since web.py does not have a pip3 package (as of this writing), you'll need to use a more complicated commandline to pull the sourcecode from GitHub and install it for you as shown below

```
$ pip3 install git+https://github.com/webpy/webpy#egg=web.py
Collecting web.py from git+https://github.com/webpy/webpy#egg=web.py
  Cloning https://github.com/webpy/webpy to /tmp/pip-build-ybf1t6/web.py
Installing collected packages: web.py
  Running setup.py install for web.py ... done
Successfully installed web.py-0.40.dev0
```

The web.py framework uses a list of pairs of paths and classes to dispatch incoming REST requests. Each request then neatly invokes a new object of the specified class and calls the GET method. There are several types of REST methods, the most common being GET and POST. The difference between GET and POST is whether the params are specified in the URL itself (GET) or in the body of the request (POST). For this exercise, we'll only use the GET method. See the listing for Exercise 12 on the following page for the full source code of rest.py. We'll launch the program on port 8000 as follows:

```
$ python3 rest2.py 8000
http://0.0.0.0:8000/
127.0.0.1:35317 - [23/Oct/2017 15:17:01] "HTTP/1.1 GET /words/count" -
200 OK
127.0.0.1:35319 - [23/Oct/2017 15:17:09] "HTTP/1.1 GET /words/freq" -
200 OK
```

The preceding output was obtained by using a curl client to send the URL params. We could have just as easily used a web browser (Chrome) or generic REST client like Postman (for Windows or Mac).

```
$ curl "localhost:8000/words/count?txt=mary+had+a+little+little+lambda"
    6

$ curl "localhost:8000/words/freq?txt=mary+had+a+little+little+lambda"
    {"lambda": 1, "little": 2, "mary": 1, "a": 1, "had": 1 }
```

And finally, our rest.py source code:

```
 1: #!/usr/bin/env python3
 2: # Exercise 12: Make your own REST server with web.py
 3: import collections
 4: import json
 5: import urllib.parse
 6: import web
 7:
 8: urls = (
 9:     '/words(.*)', 'Words'
10: )
11:
12: class Words:
13:     def GET(self, path):
14:         query = urllib.parse.unquote_plus(web.ctx.query[1:])
15:         param_dict = dict(urllib.parse.parse_qsl(query))
16:         if path == "/count":
17:             return self.word_count(param_dict['txt'])
18:         elif path == "/freq":
19:             return self.word_freq(param_dict['txt'])
21:         else:
22:             return "ERROR: bad REST path %s" % path
23:
24:     def word_count(self, line: str) -> str:   # see Lesson Two
25:         return "%d\n" % len(line.split())
26:
27:     def word_freq(self, line: str) -> str:   # see Lesson Five
28:         wordFreq = collections.Counter()
29:         for word in line.split():
30:             wordFreq[word] += 1
31:         return json.dumps(wordFreq, indent=4)
32:
33: if __name__ == "__main__":
34:     app = web.application(urls, globals())
35:     app.run()
```

Your web.py REST server is configured by passing a list of pairs of URL paths and classes to invoke, as shown in line #9. If we had more root paths other than /words, we could list them as well. You'll notice that there is a regex embedded in the URL path '/words(.*)', this means that everything following /words is gathered into the first argument of the GET method for this class. That is why on line #9 there is a path parameter which receives the results of this greedy regex. (.*) is a special regex which matches anything and everything that follows (including the slash in our URL).

The GET callback method appears on lines 13-22. If you wanted to provide an implemention for POST, DELETE, or other HTTP Methods, you could add those here too. Lines 14-15 decode the URL-encoded params and place them into a dict for easy access. Consult the Python docs about urllib for details on what it does for you. For convenience sake, I've cut-and-pasted the code from Lessons Two and Five as the word_count() and word_freq() methods.

Looking into the main() function at the end, you can see that we first create a web.py application object (line 34) and then by invoke the run() method it immediately opens the specified port for HTTP service and never returns. As GET requests come in, they are dispatched through a callback mechanism to GET() and finally word_count() or word_freq() depending on the URL path provided.

Of course, this isn't a production-ready REST server by any means. Consult the online docs of web.py for advice on integrating your web.py application into Apache Tomcat or other existing web servers you may be already using.

Python Pitfalls

As Peter Parker pointed out in *Spiderman*, "With great power comes great responsibility." Python requires such responsibility, because as an interpreted language, a great many (or some would say most) problems will not be discovered until runtime. Some pretty sticky tarpits are around so you should get yourself comfortable with them:

Comparing Strings to Numbers

Many scripting languages, including Perl and Python, are prone to make your code misbehave when you compare an integer to a literal or string expression. Example:

```
if 2 > "1":
    print("Two is bigger than one")
else:
    print("Two is less than one")

Two is less than one
```

This issue can happen most often when you read in a value from a file and forget to convert it to an integer before comparison. There are no warnings so it's your responsibility to convert at the proper time AND to handle ValueError exceptions that arise when int(x) or float(x) fails.

Code branches not yet executed will contain bugs

Just because your code works today, doesn't mean it will work tomorrow unless you have actually tested all the conditional branches (i.e. loops and if statements). Because Python is an interpreter, it won't evaluate a line until it is actually called for in the course of execution. Example:

```
numLines = 0
    :
    .
if numLines > 0:
    print(NumLines)
else:
    print("I'm ok so far")

I'm ok so far
```

In this example, there is a mis-capitalization of numLines as NumLines in the *print()* statement. Python is case-sensitive, but this error won't be reported until someday in the future when *numLines > 0*.

Catching exceptions too broadly

If you're in a hurry, you may be tempted just to catch all the errors at one time as shown below:

```
try:
       [ some code  ]
  Except Exception as e:
     print("Thing gone wrong %s" % str(e) )
```

The major problem here is that you'll be catching syntax errors, numeric conversion errors, I/O errors, and the whole kitchen sink of what can go wrong. Catching a generic exception is almost always the wrong end of the stick. Take a breath and research the right exception: OSError, ValueError, etc.

Not catching exceptions at all! ('cause it looks messy)

I have seen progammers simply wait until the code crashes here and there and only then add the exceptions like you might garnish a salad. It's always the code you didn't add the exception handler to that will crash at 4 a.m. or while you are on vacation or both. Exceptions exist to help you, so use them!

Forgetting parenthesis on a function call with no parameters

You might well be surprised to see that fh.close() closes a file but fh.close by itself does nothing.

```
fh.close
```

That is because the close method is a function *reference*, and there are many cases where you might manipulate functions as values. A function doesn't get called unless you add parenthesis to it; otherwise, it represents a reference (pointer in C++) to the method.

Forgetting to return a value from a function

This often happens when you have several different return statements in various placesin a function depending on how much or how little work you need to do for a specific case. Any time you simply use return with no value supplied, Python actually returns the special constant None. We haven't explained much about None in this book, but it represents an *empty* value, a little bit like how NULL works in SQL or the macro NULL in C/C++ languages. If execution reaches the end of a function without any return statement at all, Python handily supplies a built-in return None for you!

```
def is_big(x):
    if x > 100:
        return "big"
    elif x > 0:
        return "small"
```

Suppose we call is_big(-1), the result will be None. Unless the calling function was expecting this behavior, usually a bug will come along soon afterwards.

Use pylint to static check your code when you think it's "done"

The title of this item is not a pitfall, but rather a piece of advice: the *pylint* tool is available with most Python distributions and will "static check" your code before it runs. It may be able to help you spot a bug in advance, but first you may need to tailor its verbose reporting down to a level with which you are comfortable. By default, it is a bit over-picky about things like the length of a line of code or naming of variables, which you might agree are beside the point. Many Integrated Development Environments (IDEs) such as IntelliJ Community Edition with the PyCharm plug-in can do static checking of code as you type!

Where Do We Go From Here?

Let's do a quick re-cap of everything we visited on our one-hour tour:

- Opening and reading text files with the *for* loop
- Exception handling with *try/except*
- Using functions to compute and return values
- Basic elements of a class definition and how to call methods
- Lists and building them with the *split()* method
- Converting a list back into a string with *join()* method
- The *Counter()* and *defaultdict()* collections
- Sets and how to add and iterate through them
- How code can organically evolve from script to object-oriented style

If you went on to hour two, you also saw:

- How to count, search, and replace using regular expressions re module
- Using Python to surf the web with requests and json modules
- Launching threads to work with some level of concurrency
- Simple HTML Forms processing and integration with an external module
- Building your own REST API with web.py framework

Is this all there is? Definitely not; there are plenty of other places you can go now in your "second" hour after completing this first hour of learning. Here's a small list of recommended topics to whet your appetite for further explorations.

- List comprehension
- Reading and writing XML and YAML
- Iterators and generators
- List slicing operators
- Keyword arguments for functions
- Specialized libraries for graphics and user-interfaces

Yes, there's no limit to what you can do with Python; you'll be limited only by your curiosity and your desire to make it happen.

Recommended Resources

- **www.StackOverflow.com**: peer-reviewed source of solving common Python problems. Google searches will often land you exactly here.

- **docs.python.org**: the official documentation of Python is usually surprisingly easy to read and replete with examples.

- **www.saltycrane.com/blog**: best source of examples for common programming tasks, such datetime manipulations and conversions of container objects.

- **LearnPythonTheHardWay.org:** if you have a lot of time and want a stepwise and thorough introduction there is a free web version and purchasable digital download, textbook, and videos.

- **pythonmonk.com**: a browser-based approach where you can run and modify code right before your very eyes.

- **http://www.lynda.com/search?q=python**: source of video tutorials from 1 to 2 hours on Python and a million other topics.

About the Author

Victor R. Volkman graduated *cum laude* from Michigan Technological University with a BS in Computer Science in 1986. Since then, he has written for numerous publications, including *The C Gazette, C/C++ Users Journal, Windows Developers Journal,* and many others. Victor has thirty years of programming experience in southeastern Michigan. He has taught college-level programming courses at Washtenaw Community College and has served on the Computer Information Science (CIS) Faculty Advisory Board for more than a decade.

Volkman came to Python late in his programming career in 2011, but he is making up for lost time by teaching by example and mentoring wherever possible. With Python, he has rediscovered the joy of programming he first encountered in BASIC at age fourteen. You can find books he has written about computer programming, history, and psychology on Amazon.com.

The author can be reached by email to **victor@LHPress.com**

www.ingramcontent.com/pod-product-compliance
Lightning Source LLC
Chambersburg PA
CBHW080722220326

41520CB00056B/7363